CHRISTIAN
DEVELOPMENT
— COURSE —

Pass it on!

by DR JIM MASTER

Published by Verité CM Ltd for Jim Master

British Library Cataloguing in Publication Data
A catalogue record for this book is available from The British Library

Typesetting and Print Management by Verité CM Ltd,
Goring-by-Sea, West Sussex UK
+44 (0) 1903 241975

Printed in the UK

CONTENTS

PREFACE

In our rapidly changing society, the church needs more than ever to focus on building for the next generation so that those who come after us will be able make an impact across our nation and across the world. Sadly, these days there are many misunderstandings about training and discipling leaders in the way they should go. In writing this book I have sought, under the guidance of the Holy Spirit, to combine my experience and understanding of biblical principles, to produce something that will be of help to every Christian, not only those attending City Life International Church.

INTRODUCTION

It's a great thing to be a leader! The Apostle Paul tells us that those who aspire to leadership 'desire a good work'. Good leadership at all levels is imperative in a healthy and stable society. Leadership also involves being a good disciple and the greatest joy I get from being a senior leader is to see people develop into strong Christians; discipleship is vital to this.

The Christian Development Course is part of a very important investment in people's lives and is a way of ensuring that everyone who joins our church, whether by transfer or new converts, goes through the basic doctrine of this church so that the Word of God is not diluted in anyway and we are all singing from the same song sheet! If people are willing to accept the fundamentals of Christianity that we teach then we can continue to disciple people further. With a simple vision statement to 'pass it on!' I trust that this booklet will do just that!

Revd Dr Jim Master

NOW YOUR CHRISTIAN LIFE BEGINS

Congratulations! You have just made the best decision of your life by asking Jesus Christ into your life.

This means from now on your life is to change by nurturing and the help of other Christians. When you asked Jesus into your life you did three specific things.

You admitted your life in the past was wrong and needed to change. This is called 'repentance', which means changing your mind and actions. Your life originally didn't recognise sin as an issue and didn't know that this was disobedient towards God and would separate you from him.

> And the LORD God commanded the man, saying, 'Of every tree of the garden you may freely eat; but of the tree of the knowledge of good and evil you shall not eat, for in the day that you eat of it you shall surely die.' (Genesis 2:16–17)

Because Adam and Eve had committed sin it separated Man from God. So the only way God could bring Man back to himself was to give them an opportunity through sending His son to die on the cross to share His blood on behalf of everyone. So through this salvation became God's purpose.

This gift of salvation only comes from God which means relationship of the love for God, living in His protection and knowing that He will take you through troubled times.

You have believed that Jesus is the Son of God and to develop your new-found belief you need to learn more about the Christian faith. This means you have become a disciple of Jesus Christ and now need to

begin to learn about what it means to mature into a Christian. This is done by choosing a church where you can receive help.

You have committed yourself to learning about Christianity and once you have chosen a church and fellowship with other believers this will gently challenge you and help you on your way. A church should offer a Bible study or other facilities by which you can learn. If you're a younger person you may consider the youth group.

Reading your Bible

The first step to being a Christian is to read the Word of God, the Bible. Some people find history boring and unexciting. However, we believe the Bible is not just history; it's the living word with real life stories. The Bible is divided into two major parts: the Old and New Testaments. The Old Testament starts with Genesis with God creating the world, and goes right through until the New Testament where Jesus arrives on the scene for the very first time.

We want you to develop and grow and get to understand the fundamentals of Christianity as quickly as possible, so you begin to change your lifestyle in accordance with God. There is nothing better in life than to search for what God wants from your Christianity and know that He came to make God's kingdom available to you.

Nor is there salvation in any other, for there is no other name under heaven given among men by which we must be saved. (Acts 4:12)

Being a 'new Christian' and starting a new life with Jesus, it is recommended that you start by reading a chapter of the Bible a day. Also, you might want to meet up with friends in your church and discuss certain aspects of Scripture (Bible study).

The Bible is divided up into 66 books and these books divide into chapters and verses. For example: John 3:16 is the book of John, chapter 3, verse 16.

For God so loved the world that He gave His only begotten Son, that whoever believes in Him should not perish but have everlasting life.

When you read a passage like this, pray and mediate that the Lord will speak to you through it. We read the Bible primarily to get to know Christ, to know more about him. Also this means we come under the teaching of churches, maybe even join a Bible school, to get a full understanding of what the Bible has to offer.

Jesus came with the good news that the kingdom of heaven is near! The word 'kingdom' in the New Testament means literally the sovereign reign of God. So this is established in the hearts of men and women.

Your kingdom come. Your will be done on earth as it is in heaven. (Matthew 6:10)

So our job on this earth is to establish God's kingdom through His people. To repent is not only to have your sins forgiven, but to turn your life over to Jesus Christ that He might be the Lord of your life: that He might establish His Kingdom in you and enable you to fulfil His will.

Questions for discussion

1. What has changed since I have repented and given my life to Christ?
2. What day-to-day challenges do I face?
3. What am I reading in the Bible that will assist my life?
4. What am I doing to pray to the Lord every day?
5. Do I have a mentor to speak into my life and assist me?
6. Have I spoken to anyone about my conversion?
7. Am I going to church regularly?

HOLY SPIRIT

We believe in the Trinitarian, which is the Father, Son and Holy Spirit, and we believe the Holy Spirit is a person and not an impersonal force as some religions (like the Jehovah's Witnesses) believe.

Now that you have come to know Christ as your living Saviour I would like to introduce you to the greatest helper: the Holy Spirit.

When Christ died on the cross for your sins, He did not leave you alone, but gave you His Holy Spirit to help you live the Christian life. You may know this as it starts at the beginning of the first church in Acts 1:8:

> But you shall receive power when the Holy Spirit has come upon you; and you shall be witnesses to Me in Jerusalem, and in all Judea and Samaria, and to the end of the earth.

So we see that Jesus' instruction to His disciples is to stay in Jerusalem until they have received the Holy Spirit.

The power of the Holy Spirit will help you live the Christian life. The original word translated here as 'power' is dunamis which is the source of the word 'dynamite'! Before you were a Christian, you did things in your own strength. However, now you will do it with the dynamite strength of the Holy Spirit.

Matthew 28:18 teaches us that we have been given authority beyond human understanding.

> And Jesus came and spoke to them, saying, 'All authority has been given to Me in heaven and on earth.'

The Holy Spirit lives in you now. However, the world cannot understand this and no other religion has the gift of the Holy Spirit.

The Spirit of truth, whom the world cannot receive, because it neither sees Him nor knows Him; but you know Him, for He dwells with you and will be in you. (John 14:17)

The question is what does it mean to be filled with the Spirit?

The Holy Spirit is a person. We either have Him or we don't. In Acts 3:10 we read that people were filled with *'wonder and amazement'* at what had happened to the lame beggar when he met Peter and John. He received healing and went *'walking, leaping, and praising God'* as he entered the temple.

In Acts 13:45 we read that the multitudes were *'filled with envy'* and in Acts 13:52 that *'the disciples were filled with joy and with the Holy Spirit'.*

The Holy Spirit 'dominates' the personality of His people and 'determines our behaviour'.

So joy can dominate your personality and determine your behaviour but you need to allow the Holy Spirit to assist you with this.

In Ephesians 5:18 the Bible tells us, *'do not be drunk with wine . . . but be filled with the Spirit'!* The first thing people thought when the Holy Spirit came upon the disciples at Pentecost was that those who'd been filled had 'had too much wine'! Peter said, *'These people are not drunk, as you suppose. It's only nine in the morning!'* (Acts 2:15 NIV). Being *'filled'* is the evidence of the way you:

- walk

- talk

- smell (figuratively speaking!)

1. The way you 'walk'

I say then: Walk in the Spirit. (Galatians 5:16)

Walk in love. (Ephesian 5:2)

The word that characterises you in life is love.

Walk in light as He is in the light. (1 John 1:7)

You are to be open and not hidden away, be honest and full of integrity.

So the way you walk matters in your Christian life. People will always be observing and seeing how you react to things. The Bible says 'walk in love', which seems to be a difficult thing these days! To 'walk in light' is an amazingly powerful way to show how people will look at you and observe you. The Bible says Jesus is in the light.

2. The way you 'talk'

Out of the abundance of the heart the mouth speaks.
(Matthew 12:34)

If you want to know what is going on in someone's heart, hang around them long enough and listen to what comes out of their mouth!

When the scripture talks about the disciples being filled with His Spirit, something happens to their mouths. At the day of Pentecost they were able to speak in other tongues – other languages – as the spirit enabled them.

The Bible tells us to 'be filled with the Spirit'. But the next verse says that we are then to speak *'to one another with psalms, hymns, and songs from the Spirit. Sing and make music from your heart to the Lord'* (Ephesians 5:19 NIV).

One sign that you are filled with the Holy Spirit is that you begin to sing!

3. The way you 'smell'!

Now thanks be to God who always leads us in triumph in Christ, and through us diffuses the fragrance of His knowledge in every place. For we are to God the fragrance of Christ among those who are being saved and among those who are perishing. To the one we are the aroma of death leading to death, and to the other the aroma of life leading to life. (2 Corinthian 2:14–16)

Paul says that to God we smell of Christ and those who are saved we smell of life, but to those who are perishing, we smell of death.

The very atmosphere of our lives should speak of Christ, when filled with the Spirit. So the Holy Spirit helps us in our talking, walking and aroma we produce.

The Holy Spirit 'dominates' our personality and 'determines our behaviour'.

As a Christian you now have a faith in Christ Jesus and His Helper, the Holy Spirit, to guide you along the way, and a new power to unravel through prayer to receive and administer healing, which we shall look at in other chapters.

In the Old Testament the Hebrew word *ruach* is used, which comes from the verb 'to breathe out violently' – so could mean wind, breath or spirit. The Spirit in the Old Testament expresses itself in different ways. For example in the book of Judges it seems very military (Judges 3:10). Also in the Old Testament we see how God empowered a man, Samson, with supernatural strength.

In the New Testament in John 16:13 Jesus says, 'When He, the Spirit of truth, has come, He will guide you into all truth.' The final proof that the Spirit is a person is when Jesus says, 'He will give you another Helper, that He may abide with you forever' (John 14:16).

In the original, the word *allos* meant 'another of the same kind'. Jesus promised a person who would be the same kind as Himself.

In the book of Acts we see that the Spirit was poured on all flesh; that means everyone can experience His Spirit and not just a select few. We also see the Spirit helps in several ways:

- It is a gift from the Father (Luke 11:9–13).

- There are miracles performed by the Spirit (Matthew 12:28; Acts 1:4–8).

- The Spirit helps Christians on trial (Matthew 12:24–32; Mark 3:22–30).

In the original Greek version of the Gospel of John in chapters 14 to 16, Jesus teaches about the *paraclete*. This comes from the word parakletos, which is translated as 'comfort', 'helper' or 'advocate'. Just before He was crucified Jesus made it clear He was about to go back to the Father (14:12) who would send another Helper (14:16) who would be with them forever. He wanted to make sure that we were not orphans or without a teacher. Therefore, it was essential for the Son, Jesus, to go away so the Spirit could come. This was done for everyone!

Questions for discussion

1. What is the Trinitarian?

2. Why did God send us His Spirit?

3. Have I experienced direction from the Holy Spirit?

4. How has God's Spirit helped me?

5. Has the Holy Spirit convicted me of things that are wrong in my life?

BECOMING A PRAYING CHRISTIAN

Breakthrough in prayer

Many Christians see prayer as an additive to their lives that is often taken for granted, rather than an important primary factor to building and sustaining their faith. During this course we want you to see how essential prayer is to everything you say and do, and know that our private ministry is far more important than our public ministry. You see, what we do in private means more to God. *'Seek first the kingdom of God and His righteousness, and all these things will be added to you'* (Matthew 6:33).

The 'kingdom' is the vertical connection and the 'righteousness' is the horizontal connection between us and God, so both matter.

I would like to take you through types of prayer that may assist your daily life. On a practical note, it may be good practice to set your clock to 5–15 minutes per day and increase this as you develop your prayer life; eventually you will be praying for around 45 minutes and you'll be amazed at the breakthrough you will begin to see.

Three types of prayer:

1. Praise and worship

Definition: honour and love is conveyed in praise with words of song and music.

    a) This is the highest type of prayer in which God inhabits our praises (Psalm 22:3).

b) Common type of lifestyle.

c) It should be the first type we start with e.g. Acts 16:25–26, 1 Thessalonians 5:16, Hebrews 13:15.

d) It should be prayed for before your needs: *'And behold, a leper came and worshipped Him, saying, "Lord, if You are willing, You can make me clean"'* (Matthew 8:2).

e) It helps to bring gifts into manifestation (Acts 13:1–2).

f) Produces joy and strength (Luke 18:1).

g) God needs and meets real worshippers (Isaiah 64:5).

2. Prayer of commitment

Definition: the prayer whereby a person's cares or worries are cast upon the Lord.

a) Cast your cares on Him (1 Peter 5:7).

b) *'Cast your burdens on the LORD and He shall sustain you. He shall never permit the righteous to be moved'* (Psalm 55:22).

c) Do not fret or have anxiety (Philippians 4:6–7). This prayer type should only be prayed once, until you begin to worry again.

Used in the future for the unknown. (Matthew 6:31–33).

So it is contrary to worry:

• Worry is called evil (Matthew 6:34).

• Worry is called lack of faith (Mark 6:30).

• Worry chokes the seed of the Word from grown (Mark 4:18–19).

• Worry stops God from winning your battle (Romans 12:19).

So the prayer of commitment is to cast your burdens onto him.

3. Prayer of petition

This prayer is addressed to the Father using specific requests in Jesus' name.

> *And in that day you will ask Me nothing. Most assuredly, I say to you, whatever you ask the Father in My name He will give you.* (John 16:23)

Additional verses: Mark 7:7; 1 John 3:22; James 1:5–8.

This prayer is addressed to a specific situation. A decree of faith is addressed to a situation using Jesus' name based on a specific Bible right or promise.

4. Prayer of faith

This prayer is a decree of faith addressed to a situation using Jesus' name based on a specific 'promise' given to you or certain scriptures.

Faith will save the sick: James 5:15; Mark 11:23–24, John 14:13, 14.

The prayer of faith is often prayed once, not demanding that God change, only that the situation changes. It is also based on faith from Scriptures.

Luke 10:19–20.

2 Corinthians 1:20, every promise is 'yes'.

5. Prayer of binding and loosing

A prayer of faith using the believer's authority, permitting positive spiritual forces while resisting and stopping negative forces.

And I will give you the keys of the kingdom of heaven, and whatever you bind on earth will be bound in heaven, and whatever you loose on earth will be loosed in heaven. (Matthew 16:19)

It is usually applied against principalities and powers trying to dominate people.

1 Timothy 2:1–5; Matthew 12:29 to take authority over your life.

These are just a few types of prayer you can begin to get involved with that will help you, your family and friends. Don't just make prayer an addition, but learn to make it a lifestyle that changes the environment around you.

Questions for discussion

1. How often do I pray?

2. Do I take authority over my circumstances?

3. Do I attend prayer meetings at church?

4. What type of prayer would I use to stop worrying?

5. What would I pray in faith to see breakthrough?

6. What prayers have been answered in my life?

TYPES OF GIFTS GIVEN TO THE BODY OF CHRIST

There are a variety of gifts and ways in which they operate. There are 21 gifts broken down into 4 passages of the New Testament:

- Romans 12
- 1 Corinthians 12:8–10
- Ephesians 4:11–12
- 1 Corinthians 12:28

It is important to differentiate between these gifts and place them in their right category to avoid confusion and ascertain a better understanding of their importance within the Body.

1. Gifts of the Holy Spirit: nine gifts described in 1 Corinthians 12:1–11 (Greek words: *pneumatikos* and *charismata*).

2. Ascension gifts: five-fold ascension gifts in Ephesians 4:11; 3:7.

3. Gifts of government and leadership (Greek word: *proistemi*).

4. Gift of administration (Greek word: *kubernesis*)

5. Gifts of service: helpers (Greek words: *antilepsis* and *diakonia* Romans 12:7).

The Body has many gifts but not all have the same function.

But now God has placed the members, each one of them, in the body just as He pleased. (1 Corinthians 12:18)

The gifts are bestowed by grace, but they must be appropriated personally by faith. The Body needs each member to take their place and function as God desires.

Here is an overview of each of these categories.

Gifts of the Holy Spirit

There are nine gifts of the Holy Spirit. Paul was anxious that believers should know the source, purpose, nature and function of the gifts (1 Corinthians 12). He explained that there are varieties of gifts (*charismata* – gift of grace) but the same Spirit. And there are varieties of effects but the same God who works in all things in all persons. But to each one is given the manifestation (*phanerosis* – manifestation) of the Spirit for the common good.

Nine gifts of the Spirit are divided into three categories:

1. Gift of Revelation: wisdom, word of knowledge, discerning of spirit

2. Gift of Power: faith, healing and miracles

3. Gift of Inspiration: prophecy, tongues, interpretation of tongues

Gifts of rule/leadership/government

God calls/appoints individuals to exercise government in the church. To these individuals He gives special grace and anointing to rule and manage well the affairs of the house of God. (Ephesians 4:11). These gifts are probably the most misunderstood gifts in the church as most people think if they are blessed with one of the five-fold ministry gifts they have a governmental role in the leadership of the church.

The Greek word *presbuteros* describes this: elders, emphasising maturity (the maturity of character), or *episkopos* meaning bishops/overseers/ supervisors or better described as 'superintend' – to manage and rule over (1 Timothy 3:4).

1. *proisterni:* one who stands in front and goes before the flock (Romans 12:8).

2. *hegeomai:* govern, guide and guard the flock (Hebrews 13:7, 17).

3. *poimaino:* like a shepherd, he must feed and tend the flock (Acts 20:28).

Elders are:

• Set in the position of rule, should be trustworthy.

• Approved and appointed by laying-on of hands.

• Always appointed in plurality in each church, never singular.

• Government, known for maturity and ability.

• To give account to the Lord (Acts 14:23; 1 Timothy 3:1–7).

Gifts of administration

Administrators are essentially all-important to release others into ministry. They prepare the way for others. They make difficult things easy, heavy things bearable, and seemingly impossible things possible. The value of a God-given spiritual and faithful administrator should never be despised or underestimated.

Notice the high premium Paul places on this gift. It is mentioned in the same group of gifts as apostles, prophets, teachers and miracle workers (1 Corinthians 12:28).

The Greek word is *kubernesis* (govern) used to steer a ship according to the captain (1 Corinthians 12:28; 1 Timothy 3:8–9; Acts 6:3–6). They do not determine the destination but obey the captain's orders. A church administrator diligently attends to the practical detail to ensure that the church is kept on course to fulfil its destiny. By their serving they release others to concentrate on their priority and primary gifting.

Gifts of service and help

The Greek word *antilepsis* (1 Corinthians 12:28) meaning to lay hold of something or someone in order to help and give support. *'Do all things without complaining or disputing'* (Philippians 2:14; 1 Peter 4:9; 1 Corinthians 10:10). To give assistance to the weak and needy. It is a ministry of mercy and compassion (Romans 12:8). The ministry of helps is whole-hearted faithful service. The scope is endless. It ranges from sweeping the floor to prayer, from hospitality to ministry to the lonely and sick.

Jesus placed high rating on the ministry of helping (Matthew 25:31–46). The gifts of service may often be the menial and insignificant duties that are not highly valued by others. They are often the unseen jobs which go unnoticed that are close to the Lord's heart.

Ascension gifts (read Ephesians 4:7–16)

The ascended Christ has given five ministry gifts to the Body for the perfection of the saints and equipping the church for the work and ministry (Ephesians 4:11). They are a product of grace which Paul goes to show are gifts that come from Christ.

> *To each one of us grace was given according to the measure of Christ's gift.* (Ephesians 4:7)

When Christ ascended, as Paul said, He gave two main things: the Holy Spirit to empower us; ministry gifts to equip us.

He gives ministry gifts without consultation, without committee meetings and without board meetings! He gives them from His majestic throne. This means they are not self-appointed or chosen by the church, nor manufactured. The five-fold ministry gifts are functions not titles, they are pastor, evangelist, apostle, teacher and prophet. It's OK if you are not a prophet or an evangelist as gifts are evenly distributed. He gave 'some' to be, not all to be!

And God has appointed these in the church: first apostles, second prophets, third teachers, after that miracles, then gifts of healings, helps, administrations, varieties of tongues. Are all apostles? Are all prophets? Are all teachers? Are all workers of miracles? (1 Corinthians 12:28–29)

This means we do not have to strive to be something we are not. There is no need to feel threatened or insecure. Your gift is His gifting so we give Him the glory. We need to be careful that we understand the source of gift.

Pastors (mentioned once in the New Testament)

Pastors are the ones who feed, shield and meet the need of the church. If the whole church has pastoral gifting, then we run the risk of concentrating on the need of the flock and not the purposes of God for the overall church. Being a very good pastor doesn't necessarily make you a church builder. A pastor who is also building the church has most definitely some other gifts.

Pastors may look after their flock but they are not king of the castle! There is only one King and that is Christ Jesus.

Teachers (mentioned 13 times in New Testament)

Teachers' gifting is that of understanding and explaining the 'Word' to the people. If a church is built purely on strong teaching then the preaching will gather a crowd. But, sadly, when the teaching gift moves away the other work in the church suffers and dies. Though it is important to respect and embrace good teaching, churches cannot be built on this alone. Many churches lack evangelistic zeal and passion and therefore grow by transferral growth and not conversional i.e. people leave one church to join another, rather than joining as a result of becoming born again.

Prophets (mentioned 122 times in the New Testament)

A prophet is someone who is able to see what others do not see. Its origins come from God, whether it's foretelling or to tell forth. They have the ability to say things, sometimes what others may not want to hear!

He will speak to the people for you, and it will be as if he were your mouth and as if you were God to him. (Exodus 4:16)

Prophets lay an axe to the root; they don't beat about the bush. They demand action and speak out, often saying what the pastor never says. They provoke the church, not allowing them to settle, because they believe there is too much at stake.

They see through God's eyes, they are inquisitive, bold and sometimes fearless. Often the church is afraid of prophets.

Evangelists (mentioned 3 times in the New Testament)

An evangelist is someone who wins souls for Christ and inspires others to do the same. It is the person who carries the 'good news'. They have the ability to fill the net but are not gifted at keeping them! I believe we need evangelistic people in our church.

- John 3:5

- 1 Timothy 4:14

- Acts 1:8

- 2 Timothy 1:6

- 2 Timothy 2:15

- Romans 9:3

- 1 Samuel 1:8–16

Apostles (mentioned 83 times in the New Testament)

1. The role of the apostle as a preacher

He sent His apostles to preach the gospel of the kingdom not only with words but with demonstrations of power, signs and wonders to follow (1 Thessalonians 1:5; Mark 16:20).

2. The role of the apostle as an ambassador

Ambassadors were official representatives of Christ. Apostles are the resident officials of the highest order. He shows forth excellencies of Christ in all things to all men everywhere (1 Peter 2:9).

He is given authority over decisions in impossible situations, insurmountable conditions and demonic activities (Matthew 16:19; 18:18). The witness of their lives was the foundation of the church (Matthew 16:18).

3. The role of the apostle as a church planter

The single most outstanding evidence of an apostle is the ability to pioneer, evangelise and church plant (Acts 14:21–23). Peter exhorted the new believers to devote themselves continually and steadfastly (Acts 2:42). Paul sent Titus to Crete and Timothy to Ephesus and accepted the responsibility to see that the new believers were baptised in water and the Holy Spirit.

4. The role of the apostle to set government

They ordained elders in every church (Titus 1:5–9; Acts 14:23) to set every church in God's order.

Apostles help the church:

- To provide care
- To avoid disasters
- To bring clearer understanding

- Team roles

- To act as a court of appeal to elders

- To give direction without manipulation

5. The role of the apostle as a trainer/coach/mentor

The apostle's role is to reproduce themself in others. Peter trained the group that accompanied him, by his influence and obvious desire to see other leaders emerge (Acts 10:23).

Barnabas mentored Paul, John and Mark. Paul identified, mentored and discipled Timothy, Silas, Titus and others.

Our chief apostle is Christ (Hebrews 3:1). 'Apostle' means 'sent one'. In classical Greek, an apostle was a messenger who was sent on a mission to a king or emperor to deal with a specific mission. In fact, during the reign of Alexander the Great there is a record of such terminology. Alexander sent out a naval task force on his behalf; the task force was called 'Apostolic Mission'. The naval commander was called an apostle. His mission was to conquer and govern in the name of a king. It is a part of the five-fold ministry. He is a problem solver. The apostle develops the Body of the church after a number of years.

Often apostles gave through all the gifting, and had insight into everything. Paul took seventeen years to develop – three years in Arabia, fourteen years in other ministry. He was a master builder (Ephesians 2:20).

It is the apostle that is the chief cornerstone. To be or work with an apostle should be a delight.

5

MARRIAGE AND DIVORCE

Marriage is a sacred union between a man and woman, ordained by God. Therefore, when two people marry in the sight of God they become 'one flesh'.

> *Marriage is honourable among all, and the bed undefiled; but fornicators and adulterers God will judge.* (Hebrews 13:4)

> *And the LORD God said, 'It is not good that man should be alone; I will make him a helper comparable to him.* (Genesis 2:18)

> *Therefore a man shall leave his father and mother and be joined to his wife, and they shall become one flesh.* (Genesis 2:24)

> *But from the beginning of the creation, God 'made them male and female.' 'For this reason a man shall leave his father and mother and be joined to his wife, and the two shall become one flesh'; so then they are no longer two, but one flesh. Therefore what God has joined together, let not man separate.* (Mark 10:6–9)

> *'For this reason a man shall leave his father and mother and be joined to his wife, and the two shall become one flesh.' This is a great mystery, but I speak concerning Christ and the church. Nevertheless let each one of you in particular so love his own wife as himself, and let the wife see that she respects her husband.* (Ephesians 5:31–33)

> *It is good for a man not to touch a woman. Nevertheless, because of sexual immorality, let each man have his own wife, and let each woman have her own husband. Let the husband render to his wife*

the affection due her, and likewise also the wife to her husband. The wife does not have authority over her own body, but the husband does. And likewise the husband does not have authority over his own body, but the wife does. Do not deprive one another except with consent for a time, that you may give yourselves to fasting and prayer; and come together again so that Satan does not tempt you because of your lack of self-control. (1 Corinthians 7:1–5)

Wives, likewise, be submissive to your own husbands, that even if some do not obey the word, they, without a word, may be won by the conduct of their wives. (1 Peter 3:1)

Husbands, likewise, dwell with them with understanding, giving honour to the wife, as to the weaker vessel, and as being heirs together of the grace of life, that your prayers may not be hindered. (1 Peter 3:7)

More than 50 per cent of all marriages end in divorce! Cohabiting has become the norm. In 1995 studies showed half of all people under the age of 40 lived together out of wedlock. In 1998 only 68 per cent of children were living with their biological married parents.

Furthermore it has been said, 'Whoever divorces his wife, let him give her a certificate of divorce.' But I say to you that whoever divorces his wife for any reason except sexual immorality causes her to commit adultery; and whoever marries a woman who is divorced commits adultery. (Matthew 5:31–32)

Now to the married I command, yet not I but the Lord: A wife is not to depart from her husband. But even if she does depart, let her remain unmarried or be reconciled to her husband. And a husband is not to divorce his wife. But to the rest I, not the Lord,

say: If any brother has a wife who does not believe, and she is willing to live with him, let him not divorce her. And a woman who has a husband who does not believe, if he is willing to live with her, let her not divorce him. For the unbelieving husband is sanctified by the wife, and the unbelieving wife is sanctified by the husband; otherwise your children would be unclean, but now they are holy. But if the unbeliever departs, let him depart; a brother or a sister is not under bondage in such cases. But God has called us to peace. For how do you know, O wife, whether you will save your husband? Or how do you know, O husband, whether you will save your wife? (1 Corinthians 7:10–16)

Infidelity, adultery and sexual immorality

Adultery is a violation of the covenant of marriage. It involves wilful sexual immorality with a person to whom one is not married. It is a sin against God and a violation of the marriage vows. It is a threat to the family and erosion on society. Adultery is not only sinning against God and the Holy Spirit but also against one's spouse and one's self.

You shall not commit adultery. (Exodus 20:14)

Do you not know that the unrighteous will not inherit the kingdom of God? Do not be deceived. Neither fornicators, nor idolaters, nor adulterers, nor homosexuals, nor sodomites, nor thieves, nor covetous, nor drunkards, nor revilers, nor extortioners will inherit the kingdom of God. (1 Corinthians 6:9–10)

Whoever commits adultery with a woman lacks understanding; he who does so destroys his own soul. Wounds and dishonour he will get, and his reproach will not be wiped away. (Proverbs 6:32–33)

Pre-marital sex is wrong

For this is the will of God, your sanctification: that you should abstain from sexual immorality; that each of you should know how to possess his own vessel in sanctification and honour, not in passion of lust, like the Gentiles who do not know God; that no one should take advantage of and defraud his brother in this matter, because the Lord is the avenger of all such, as we also forewarned you and testified. For God did not call us to uncleanness, but in holiness. (1 Thessalonians 4:3–7)

Flee sexual immorality. Every sin that a man does is outside the body, but he who commits sexual immorality sins against his own body. Or do you not know that your body is the temple of the Holy Spirit who is in you, whom you have from God, and you are not your own? For you were bought at a price; therefore, glorify God in your body and in your spirit, which are God's. (1 Corinthians 6:18–20)

Same sex marriage according to the Bible

You shall not lie with a male as with a woman. It is an abomination. (Leviticus 18:22)

Do you not know that the unrighteous will not inherit the kingdom of God? Do not be deceived. Neither fornicators, nor idolaters, nor adulterers, nor homosexuals, nor sodomites, nor thieves, nor covetous, nor drunkards, nor revilers, nor extortioners will inherit the kingdom of God. And such were some of you. But you were washed, but you were sanctified, but you were justified in the name of the Lord Jesus and by the Spirit of our God. (1 Corinthians 6:9–11)

Adultery can be forgiven

Jesus forgave the women caught up in adultery.

If we confess our sins, He is faithful and just to forgive us our sins and to cleanse us from all unrighteousness. (1 John 1:9)

Therefore, if anyone is in Christ, he is a new creation; old things have passed away; behold, all things have become new. (2 Corinthians 5:17)

He who covers his sins will not prosper, but whoever confesses and forsakes them will have mercy. (Proverbs 28:13)

Five steps for those whose marriage is under attack:

1. Know God's will for your marriage

It is not God's will for any marriage to end in divorce.

And I say to you, whoever divorces his wife, except for sexual immorality, and marries another, commits adultery; and whoever marries her who is divorced commits adultery.(Matthew 19:9)

Therefore a man shall leave his father and mother and be joined to his wife, and they shall become one flesh. (Genesis 2:24)

2. Recognise that you are in a spiritual battle

For we do not wrestle against flesh and blood, but against principalities, against powers, against the rulers of the darkness of this age, against spiritual hosts of wickedness in the heavenly places. (Ephesians 6:12)

3. Refuse to react to circumstances

Don't react to verbal attack or other negative situations – that will fight fire with fire! Angry words are met with angry words, bitterness and unforgiveness sets in.

4. Use your authority of binding and loosing

And I will give you the keys of the kingdom of heaven, and whatever you bind on earth will be bound in heaven, and whatever you loose on earth will be loosed in heaven. (Matthew 16:19)

In prayer, bind the spirit hindering your relationship. Bind the spirit of anger, rejection, fear, bitterness, unforgiveness and contention. Begin to release the spirit of love, forgiveness, peace and trust.

5. Persevere and don't give up!

Refuse to listen to the enemy. Divorce or separation is not the answer. God has made it possible for you to live a victorious Christian life in which you can take a firm stand.

The Bible tells us that we are to love one another, so when it comes to people who feel they want to get divorced we do as much as we can to assist and help them to remain in their marriage. Every situation is different and we take this very seriously and deal with each situation separately.

When it comes to marriage of the same sex we explain clearly that we believe marriage is between a man and woman. However, we continue to show love and acceptance of the individual without compromising our beliefs.

WATER BAPTISM

If you are reading this you probably have just become a Christian and have decided to be baptised.

We believe that a person needs to understand and know they want to be baptised and live their lives in harmony with Christ. Also, our belief is that a person is to be totally immersed in water as a symbol of Christ being buried and raised from the dead. It is during this time we would love to hear your testimony of how you came to Christ. But, first, here are some details on water baptism.

Definition

A transliteration of the Greek word *baptisma*, meaning 'an immersion' (baptizo means 'baptise' or 'immerse'). Every known instance of the use of baptisma and its cognates found in first-century literature either demands or permits the word to be understood as 'immerse'. It is not unequivocally provable that the word ever allowed for anything less than immersion in the period in which the New Testament was penned. Nevertheless, many churches pour or sprinkle water over would-be subjects of baptism, and call that pouring or sprinkling by the term 'baptism'.

Now you are a Christian it is time for you to be baptised. This is something you do not have to think about too much because it is more to do with the action that symbolises your commitment to Christ that outwardly demonstrates what you inwardly believe.

Water baptism is a symbolic burial, by which the new Christian publicly declares they have died, and are now beginning a new life in Christ.

> *Therefore we are buried with Him by baptism into death, that just as Christ was raised from the dead by the glory of the Father, even so we also should walk in newness of life.* (Romans 6:4)

> *In Him you were also . . . buried with him in baptism, in which you also were raised with Him through faith in the working of God, who raised Him from the dead.* (Colossians 2:11–12)

You never read of an unbaptised Christian anywhere in the Bible. In fact, baptism immediately followed a person's salvation. They didn't see it as something to be delayed or put off. Let's take a look at some of the conversions described in the book of Acts.

> *Then Peter said to them, 'Repent, and let every one of you be baptised in the name of Jesus Christ for the remission of sins; and you shall receive the gift of the Holy Spirit.'* (Acts 2:38)

> *Then those who gladly received his word were baptised.*
> (Acts 2:41)

In Acts 8:26–40 we read the account of Phillip leading the Ethiopian eunuch to Christ. As they finish their discussion, the eunuch enthusiastically asks, 'What hinders me from being baptised?' to which Phillip replies, *'If you believe with all your heart, you may.'* Then they come to a body of water, and Philip promptly baptises him.

In the Christian faith, when people have decided to believe and have given their heart to the Lord and received forgiveness of sins, then they are fully immersed in water.

Water baptism is a testimony to your family and friends that your old life is behind and your new life is beginning!

Baptism is a commandment not a suggestion!

Go therefore and make disciples of all nations, baptising them in the name of the Father and of the Son and of the Holy Spirit, teaching them to observe all things that I have commanded you; and lo, I am with you always, even to the end of the age.
(Matthew 28:19–20)

Jesus was also baptised.

Then Jesus came from Galilee to John at the Jordan to be baptised by him. And John tried to prevent Him, saying, 'I need to be baptised by You, and are You coming to me?' But Jesus answered and said to him, 'Permit it to be so now, for thus it is fitting for us to fulfil all righteousness.' Then he allowed Him. When He had been baptised, Jesus came up immediately from the water; and behold, the heavens were opened to Him, and He saw the Spirit of God descending like a dove and alighting upon Him. (Matthew 3:13–16)

Practical instructions for your baptism

1. When you come to your baptism make sure you bring two sets of clothing.

2. Make sure the clothing you wear is not going to be see through when wet!

3. Please wear trousers (men and women).

4. As you come out of the water please ensure you have a friend who will hand you a towel and assist you to the changing area.

Questions for discussion

1. Why do I want to be baptised?

2. What is my testimony about being a Christian?

3. What does baptism means to me?

4. Baptism does not give me salvation. Why?

5. How will I increase my knowledge once I have been baptised?

6. How am I going to witness to others about what has happened to me?

7. Have I chosen a prayer partner to help me be disciplined in my Christian life?

TONGUES AND THE HOLY SPIRIT

As a new believer, you may find this subject a little challenging! Most people worshipping at Pentecostal churches have received a gift from the Holy Spirit that is the gift of tongues. Some find this phenomenon a bit complex but it's worth exploring.

The gift of tongues doesn't make you better than anyone else, but it can help you become a better person! There are three instances in the book of Acts where speaking in tongue is mentioned: Acts 2; Acts 10:44–46; Acts 19:6.

In Acts 10:44–46 Peter went to Cornelius, the first Gentile who began to speak in tongues. In this instance the Holy Spirit came on all men and the gift was poured out onto the Gentiles. They were amazed at speaking in tongues and praising God. Paul came to Ephesus and found twelve men being baptised by John. Paul asked them if they had received the Holy Spirit and they responded that had not heard of this.

> *When Paul had laid hands on them, the Holy Spirit came upon them, and they spoke with tongues and prophesied.* (Acts 19:6)

So these are instances where speaking in tongues is mentioned in the book of Acts. Like me – I received tongues when I gained knowledge of this.

What is this phenomenon and can I receive it?

A hundred year ago 99 per cent of Christians made the assumption that 'tongues' was only something that happened in the time of Jesus. It was in the late 1900s that a woman in Scotland began to speak in tongues, a totally new phenomenon! People went to visit her and it was the beginning

of a revival and the speaking in tongues in this country. In 1906, Azusa Street, California, saw a revival that brought about the beginning of the Pentecostal movement and later the charismatic movement.

They were all filled with the Holy Spirit and began to speak with other tongues, as the Spirit gave them utterance. (Acts 2:4)

While Peter was still speaking these words, the Holy Spirit fell upon all those who heard the word. And those of the circumcision who believed were astonished, as many as came with Peter, because the gift of the Holy Spirit had been poured out on the Gentiles also. For they heard them speak with tongues and magnify God. (Acts 10:44–46)

'Tongues' is a gift given by God and you can receive it anytime.

Paul says, *'I thank my God I speak with tongues more than you all.* (1 Corinthians 14:18–19)

Speaking in tongues has a personal role; it edifies you:

He who speaks in tongues edifies himself, but he who prophecies edifies the church. (1 Corinthians 14:4)

Speaking in tongues has a public role:

How is it then, brethren? Whenever you come together, each of you has a psalm, has a teaching, has a tongue, has a revelation, has an interpretation. (1 Corinthians 14:26–28)

So let us receive this gift and use it together publicly and in private to edify ourselves. I pray you receive this gift.

TITHES AND OFFERINGS

Tithes and offerings has always been an essential part of the growth of the church which sees God's blessings bestowed upon individuals as well as the overall church. It is one of the most powerful tools that God has given to Christians that He lovingly expects us to abide by in order to see His kingdom grow and His people blessed. I have been tithing for around thirty years now and have seen provisions given to my family continuously. My highest single outgoing is my tithe as I see my other bills coming down!

In this session I have tried to break down the purpose of tithes and offerings so that you can better understand the principles and mistakes people often make, especially when putting their tithes in the wrong place!

Why tithe

People are often amazed when they realise that the Lord is interested in our finance, as He only wants the best for us in every area of our lives living by His kingdom principles.

A famous Christian writer wrote: 'The right attitude to money reveals your attitude to God and produces the right results.'

Money plays a very important part in everyone's lives. If our money is not managed right our lives are not managed right. So we can't pretend it doesn't matter!

The Bible uses a word 'tithe'. The first record of this is in Genesis 14:17–20.

It started with a tenth of a person's income which would be given to God (His church). This was under grace and not under law. Abraham had just

won a great battle over certain kings, and in winning the battle he had gathered a great quantity of material.

A man called Melchizedek was a priest of God Most High, who blessed Abraham. Abraham reciprocated after winning the battle and gave 10 per cent back to Melchizedek.

Hebrews 7:4–10 in the New Testament recounts this episode. It says that Abraham was a lesser person who blessed a High Priest Melchizedek. Today we do the same but give this to the church, which is the kingdom of heaven.

What happens when you tithe

Read Malachi 3:8–12 and you will find that there are certain protective provisions that start to happen when you tithe.

We have established that a tithe is 10 per cent of your income. Also it is 'Holy unto the Lord'. It is assigned to the kingdom. So if you don't tithe it will end up elsewhere. Most Christians I meet say when they tithe their own money goes a long way but those who don't say 'where has my money gone'!

Tithing becomes a covenant token between you and God that subsequently releases blessings.

Where the tithe goes

Malachi was speaking to leaders who, after a while, had not tithed, so God gets serious with them. Malachi 3:10 speaks about the 'store house'. This is basically two things:

- It's the place where you worship and get fed, in other words the church you regularly attend.

- It's where we obtain the seed we sow for the future.

Therefore Christians ought to bring tithes to the store house (church) they have joined. I can't tithe into another store house as it would lose its status and become an offering not a tithe!

You are cursed with a curse for you have robbed me, even this whole nation. (Malachi 3:9)

The Bible uses different words that are translated as 'curse'. However, here the verb 'curse' in Hebrew, arar, means to 'render powerless'. So there are consequences which render you powerless. In other words, you won't live a totally fulfilled life with an open heaven. Let's look at this 'fulfilled life' in relation to God's promises.

If we look again at Malachi 3:10 we read:

If I will not open for you the windows of heaven.

So if I tithe the windows of heaven will open on me. It is the only scripture that says the windows of heaven will open on you.

And pour out for you such blessing that there will not be room enough to receive it.

It is exciting when the Scriptures say that you will have more than enough to receive it.

And in verse 11:

And I will rebuke the devourer for your sakes.

As you tithe you are advancing the kingdom and the devil does not like that. So we rebuke him as we give towards the Lord.

So that he will not destroy the fruit of your ground.

So whatever work you have done in the past, planted seeds will not be destroyed or come to nothing.

Nor shall the vine fail to bear fruit for you in the field.

Again, there's going to be a harvest in your life; things will multiply and increase.

And verse 12:

'And all nations will call you blessed, for you will be a delightful land,' says the LORD of hosts.

People will wonder why you are beginning to be blessed over those around you. There may be adverse conditions, but you will produce fruit.

Offerings

Over and above the tithe, we give offerings. Where tithing brings God's promises and protection over certain things, multiplication comes when you give over and above your tithe! For example, I might want to give to the building fund or a project for disadvantaged children abroad. This is known as 'sowing and reaping'. You can't sow and reap and not tithe. You tithe first then sow and reap. In my experience the most generous people who give with a joyful heart prosper the most.

No one is forced to tithe or give offerings (sow and reap) but you are doing yourself a disservice if you don't, as this is one of God's main kingdom principles.

Questions for discussion

1. Where do my 10 per cent tithes go?

2. If I don't tithe what is my money going towards?

3. What is the difference between an offering and a tithe?

4. What promises does God make when we tithe?

5. Is the blessing just for me?

6. How well must I learn to steward my remaining 90 per cent?

7. When should I tithe?

8. Am I living in God's blessings?

HEALING

When you feel hurt, it's not only your emotions that can be affected, but hurt normally goes deeper within the spirit, into the inner man. If an individual is repeatedly hurt over a period of time, then their spirit will eventually become weak and broken. This subject is something that can help those who have been hurt in their lifetime. It's not instantaneous in all cases but a journey that takes time precept by precept. As a Christian there will be things you can deal with that you never thought you could before.

> *The spirit of a man will sustain him in sickness, but who can bear a broken spirit?* (Proverbs 18:14)

There are those who've been physically or verbally abused and those who have been neglected and rejected by their parents throughout their childhood. These are people who experience hurt after hurt. This also includes husbands or wives who have been verbally abused by their partners resulting in broken spirits.

Jesus came to heal the brokenhearted and to heal those who have been bruised and crushed. He is the only one who can heal a broken spirit.

> *The Spirit of the LORD is upon Me, because He has anointed Me to preach the gospel to the poor; He has sent Me to heal the brokenhearted, to proclaim liberty to the captives and recovery of sight to the blind, to set at liberty those who are oppressed.* (Luke 4:18)

45

Those who are born again can be strengthened by God's divine Spirit

Do you not know that you are the temple of God and that the Spirit of God dwells in you? (1 Corinthians 3:16)

So, as a result of His Spirit living within us, we are more than able to endure and overcome every trial, circumstance, sickness, tragedy, etc. that may come into our lives.

By His Spirit within us, our spirits are supernaturally empowered! The life of Christ flows through us and we are able to live in total wholeness – spirit, body and soul.

He would grant you, according to the riches of His glory, to be strengthened with might through His Spirit in the inner man. (Ephesians 3:16)

The spiritual strength available to Christians is a measure, not according to our weaknesses, need, or even according to what we can think or comprehend, but according to the abundance of His glory for all that God is and has.

So how do you deal with deep wounds that have affected you for years? Well, the first thing to do is to pray and ask for God's help to enable you to do certain things:

1. Recognise the areas where you have become wounded in your spirit. This becomes a key for breakthrough and allows for potential of healing. If you fail to recognise the root, you will only deal with the symptom and not the cause.

2. Allow God to heal you. That is easier said than done, you might be saying. However, when you recognise a higher and awesome Being greater than yourself, you come to realise that you don't have to do things in your own strength. Jesus by 'His' Spirit in

you, needs to be activated; your human spirit – however much you try by yourself – will always fail! Therefore, you need a greater power to help you and heal you.

3. Guard your spirit from further wounds. It's so easy to let the past dictate your future, I have to learn to protect and guard my heart. Only God truly knows what I have been through, so I let Him guard me from any further wounds.

Choose to be a victor . . . not a victim!

The very moment you are mistreated, hurt or wounded, try to refuse to react in the flesh and refuse to give Satan an opportunity to gain a stronghold in your life.

> *For he is God's minister to you for good. But if you do evil, be afraid; for he does not bear the sword in vain; for he is God's minister, an avenger to execute wrath on him who practises evil.* (Romans 13:14)

Don't make way for your flesh to react in anger, self-pity, bitterness, resentment, unforgiveness or revenge towards those who have hurt you.

If you are holding on to feelings of anger, resentment or bitterness towards someone who has hurt you, then take control and confess it openly to God as He is the only who can heal your wounded spirit.

Don't try to hide your feelings from God. He knows your innermost feelings and thoughts.

Trust in God for complete healing and restoration

Refuse to hold onto the past! Satan will use your past hurts, sins and failures to drag you down and keep you from experiencing the fullness of God's blessings. Forget the past and take hold of the future!

For the weapons of our warfare are not carnal but mighty in God for pulling down strongholds, casting down arguments and every high thing that exalts itself against the knowledge of God, bringing every thought into captivity to the obedience of Christ. (2 Corinthians 10:4–5)

Once you have taken authority over your feelings and have submitted to the Holy Spirit, commit yourself into the hands of God and trust Him to complete the healing and restoration process.

'For I will restore health to you and heal you of your wounds,' says the LORD, 'because they called you an outcast saying: "This is Zion; no one seeks her."' (Jeremiah 30:17)

Major ways in which our spirit becomes wounded, weakened, overwhelmed and broken

1. Sin wounds and weakens our spirit

For my iniquities have gone over my head; like a heavy burden they are too heavy for me. My wounds are foul and festering because of my foolishness. I am troubled, I am bowed down greatly; I go mourning all the day long. (Psalm 38:4–6)

I am feeble and severely broken; I groan because of the turmoil of my heart. (Psalm 38:8)

When we allow sin to remain in our lives and fail to confess this and gain victory over it, then it can cause spiritual depression and a sense of guilt and remorse.

Sin which is not confessed will only drag you down, drain you of your peace and joy, hinder your communion with God, and give Satan the opportunity to keep you feeling defeated.

We must be quick to acknowledge when we have sinned, by confessing our sin and allowing Christ to cleanse and heal us.

If I regard iniquity in my heart, The LORD will not hear. (Psalm 66:18)

If we confess our sins, He is faithful and just to forgive us our sins and to cleanse us from all unrighteousness. (1 John 1:9)

2. Our spirit becomes overwhelmed by the wounds from our enemies

They have all turned aside, they have together become corrupt; there is none who does good, no, not one. Have all the workers of iniquity no knowledge, who eat up my people as they eat bread, and do not call on the LORD? (Psalm 14:3–4)

Oh, that the salvation of Israel would come out of Zion! When the LORD brings back the captivity of His people, let Jacob rejoice and Israel be glad. (Psalm 14:7)

Sometimes our lives are like King David's where it seems the persecution of our enemies is so intense and so persistent that our spirit feels overwhelmed; we are at a point of losing hope and filled with despair.

Our spirits are wounded and we need to be renewed, refreshed and to receive a supernatural impartation of God's power.

It is so easy to get spiritually weary and feel you cannot go another step but . . . God's promise to you is:

'For I will restore health to you and heal you of your wounds,' says the LORD, 'because they called you an outcast saying: "This is Zion; no one seeks her."' (Jeremiah 30:17)

3. Anger

It is so easy to react in anger and flow from the mouth! If you yield to this anger and do not recognise it for what it is, it will take hold and eventually destroy you.

Brood of vipers! How can you, being evil, speak good things? For out of the abundance of the heart the mouth speaks. (Matthew 12:34)

So we will lash out in anger and bitter words! It is important to stay on guard so anger does not remain in our heart.

'Be angry, and do not sin': do not let the sun go down on your wrath, nor give place to the devil. (Ephesians 4:26–27)

You have heard that it was said to those of old, 'You shall not murder, and whoever murders will be in danger of the judgment.' But I say to you that whoever is angry with his brother without a cause shall be in danger of the judgment. And whoever says to his brother, 'Raca!' shall be in danger of the council. But whoever says, 'You fool!' shall be in danger of hell fire. Therefore if you bring your gift to the altar, and there remember that your brother has something against you, leave your gift there before the altar, and go your way. First be reconciled to your brother, and then come and offer your gift. (Matthew 5:21–24)

Here Jesus compared harbouring anger and malice in our spirits to murder! When we allow anger to remain in us, it will eventually erupt through bitter, harsh words spoken to hurt and destroy others. Get rid of all anger in your heart!

4. Bitterness

It is important to guard against bitterness; it will take hold in our spirits . . . eating away at us like a deadly cancerous growth spreading throughout the body and killing healthy cells.

When someone's spirit is deeply wounded, bitterness will immediately try to take root . . . if we allow it. The root of bitterness distorts our judgment and blocks us from healing.

If you harbour bitterness and resentment towards someone else, it cuts off the relationship with that person and with God.

Bitterness causes torment and bears bitter fruit. You can't hide it, it is a deadly poison which spreads and defiles people and makes them unfit to stand before God (Hebrews 12:15).

Don't allow a trace to remain.

5. Unforgiveness

When we live with unforgiveness in our spirit towards those who have hurt us, it blocks the healing process; it hinders our relationship with God and we'll remain defeated.

True forgiveness is the key to being set free and being healed of wounds. When we are hurt, we have a choice: either hold onto our unforgiveness and remain a victim, or choose to forgive and become whole once again.

The type of forgiveness we are to have towards others should be in accordance with the forgiveness we have received from Christ.

> *Therefore, as the elect of God, holy and beloved, put on tender mercies, kindness, humility, meekness, longsuffering; bearing with one another, and forgiving one another, if anyone has a complaint against another; even as Christ forgave you, so you also must do.* (Colossians 3:12–13)

In 2 Corinthians Jesus made it very clear that unless we are willing to forgive one another, we cannot be forgiven. Our forgiveness and acceptability by God depends upon the forgiveness we have to one another.

It is time to rid ourselves of any unforgiveness and pour out to God all the pain and hurt that you feel.

For if you forgive men their trespasses, your heavenly Father will also forgive you. But if you do not forgive men their trespasses, neither will your Father forgive your trespasses. (Matthew 6:14–15)

So the end result is to be a forgiving person, knowing that we will also be forgiven. I know how hard it may be to forgive someone who has abused you and ridiculed you verbally or physically, but through your inner strength in Christ you can forgive that person, so that person will end up forgiving someone else. That is the real reason why Jesus died for you.

Questions for discussion

1. What am I doing to make my journey with forgiveness easier?

2. Do I still think about what happened to me in the past?

3. Am I set free from all guilt and shame of the past?

4. Have I told the person that I have forgiven them?

5. Do I pray for those who hurt me?

6. Have I taken the next step to increasing my Christian life?

7. Have I given my testimony to others?

GROWING YOUR FAITH

Faith comes by hearing and doing!

Now faith is the substance of things hoped for, the evidence of things not seen. (Hebrews 11:1)

Faith is 'now', which means it is alive and powerful. It is a title deed of that which is unseen and, though it is invisible, it becomes settled on the inside. We believe in God even though we can't see Him. In Romans 10:17 it is written:

So then faith comes by hearing, and hearing by the word of God.

So when you hear God's Word your faith has the potential to increase. So, if your faith is low, increase it by the Word of God. The 'Word' gives us revelation of things that are not yet seen, that's why we need to increase God's Word by meditating on it every day.

The Spirit of faith is defined by the apostle Paul in 2 Corinthians 4:13:

And since we have the same spirit of faith, according to what is written, 'I believed and therefore I spoke,' we also believe and therefore speak . . .

James adds another dimension to faith in James 2:14–26. In addition to believing, receiving and confessing the promise of God, there must be some works or corresponding actions.

Faith without works is dead!

What does it profit, my brethren, if someone says he has faith but does not have works? Can faith save him? If a brother or sister is naked and destitute of daily food, and one of you says to them, 'Depart in peace, be warmed and filled,' but you do not give them the things which are needed for the body, what does it profit? (James 2:14–16)

There needs to be practical work involved and followed through or corresponding actions to align with what you are believing for and speaking into. This is why City Life Church has a work in India and Africa, to name just a couple, to show our faith in action.

James goes onto say in verse 17:

Thus also faith by itself, it does not have works, is dead.

'Works' as used here means 'corresponding action' – it is something you do in agreement with what you are believing and speaking. However, in Galatians Paul says that we are saved by faith and not by works. Therefore we need faith to come to Christ but this isn't the only thing we need!

Strong faith is often seen in the works we produce and James talks about 'hearing and doing' the word (James 2:20–21). An example is when Abraham had to sacrifice his son, because it was accounted righteousness and he was called a 'friend' of God. Even though Abraham was given an instruction beyond our thinking he was willing to sacrifice his own son in order to obey God.

Faith without actions

You see, with much faith comes much responsibility and sacrifice, but also great rewards! Faith is something which grows. In Luke 5:18 we

find the story of the paralysed man carried by four of his friends into the presence of Jesus so he could be healed.

> *Then behold, men brought on a bed a man who was paralysed whom they sought to bring in and lay before Him.*

It would take the will of a paralysed person to let four men carry him to the healing meeting. He did what he could do, and that was either to influence the four to take him to Jesus, or to agree with their suggestion to take him to Jesus.

> *And when they could not find how they might bring him in, because of the crowd, they went up on the housetop and let him down with his bed through the tiling into the midst before Jesus. When He saw their faith, He said to him, 'Man, your sins are forgiven you.'*
> (Luke 5:19–20)

You can see faith!

When four Jewish faces looked down through a hole in the roof, Jesus saw their faith. Their faith ripped a hole in the roof. Jesus' response was: 'Which is easier to say, "Your sins are forgiven you" or to say, "Rise up and walk"?' (Luke 5:23). In other words, 'What difference, does it make whether I say you are forgiven or you are healed?' because the Son of man has the power to do both!

When people see you act on the Word of God because you love God with all of your heart, you will also see a difference in your life. For some of us it takes time to grow our faith and see a difference and it is often to do with how bold we are in taking that step.

> *'Daughter your faith has made you well. Go in peace, and be healed of your affliction.'* (Mark 5:34).

This healing happened simply because a woman believed that to touch Jesus' garment would be enough. Sometimes doing something which

seems so trivial can have a tremendous impact! This is exactly what faith is. It is your bold step that can change things! We learn from this that Jesus looks at your heart and what you do.

> *For I say, through the grace given to me, to everyone who is among you, not to think of himself more highly than he ought to think, but to think soberly, as God has dealt to each one a measure of faith.*
> (Romans 12:3)

We see here there are varying measures of faith. Paul says that we ought 'to think' so faith can grow in our life. Faith often comes with humility. If we humble ourselves before God we will see a multitude of things happen which will increase our faith.

Always look back at a reference to when God did amazing things for you and use that experience for your next breakthrough. Remember, if He did it then, He can do it now! That's how my faith has built up over the years. Also, churches that preach messages on spiritual growth and challenge us to the very core will increase our faith.

Questions for discussion

1. When was the last time I saw God move through my faith?

2. How would I define faith?

3. Has my faith grown in the last few years?

4. Have people around helped my faith?

5. How do I help people through their faith?

ABOUT THE AUTHOR

Revd Jim Master was born in Calcutta and shortly after his birth lived in France. At a young age his family finally settled in west London. His mother being half Portuguese, half British and his father from an Asian background, both having mixed faiths, decided it was OK to send him to a Baptist church! This is where he began his Christian journey. At the age of 10 he gave his heart to the Lord and started preaching the gospel at the age of 13. Whilst at high school, he became leader of the Christian Union and led many to Christ. This was only the beginning!

His father encouraged him to attend college and study electronics; this eventually led him into a national telecommunications company. It was during this time that he met his wife Giovanna.

Two years into working at the telecommunications company, he became a junior manager and worked up to a director's position in charge of a large team of staff whose job it was to write Street Works law for the government. During the same time, he was ministering as a lay preacher in the Baptist Church when, in his early twenties, he experienced something new and exciting in his faith as he was baptised in the Holy Spirit. This is where things really began to take off as he experienced God's awesome anointing on his life. Leading a youth group at the church whilst still in secular employment, he witnessed many young people coming to Christ and, after serving many faithful years in the Baptist arena, felt God leading him into the Pentecostal churches of the Assemblies of God.

Studying is an integral part of Jim's life and his desire to know more about God and equip himself for God's calling led him to study at a higher education level, achieving a BA in Bible Studies, MA in Conflict

Management and Doctorate in Religious Studies. His first experience as a part-time Senior Pastor was at a church in Isleworth, Middlesex. A few years later he became Associate Pastor for a large church in Wembley, London. Having served five years at Wembley he then went on to become Senior Pastor of City Life Christian Church, a vibrant, growing church in Sheffield where he is currently based.

He has had the privilege of sitting on several committees including holding the office of Administrator for the Assemblies of God in London. He was also an executive member of Dr Morris Cerullo's Mission to London, where he was involved in leading the prayer meeting. In addition to lecturing at leadership courses, he was recently nominated to head up a prayer team in the Yorkshire area.

Jim has been married to Giovanna for 30 years and together they have two adult children, Carmelina 30, and Angelo 28. They currently reside in Sheffield.

NOTES

....

....

....

....

....

....

....

....

....

....

....

....

....

....

....

NOTES

NOTES

NOTES

NOTES

NOTES